THOMAS
THE TANK ENGINE

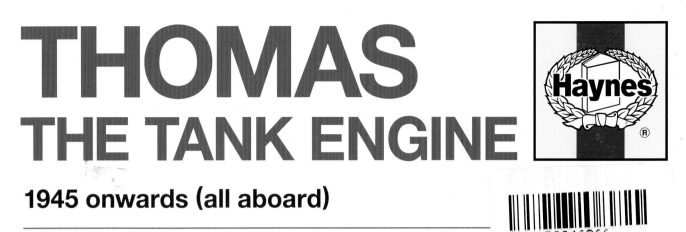

1945 onwards (all aboard)

Owners' Workshop Manual

THOMAS

First published in October 2009
Reprinted in paperback in November 2015

by arrangement with Egmont UK Limited,
239 Kensington High Street, London W8 6SA

Thomas the Tank Engine & Friends™

CREATED BY BRITT ALLCROFT

Based on the Railway Series by the Reverend W Awdry
© 2009 Gullane (Thomas) LLC. A HIT Entertainment company.
Thomas the Tank Engine & Friends and Thomas & Friends
are trademarks of Gullane (Thomas) Limited.
Thomas the Tank Engine & Friends and Design is Reg. U.S.
Pat. & Tm. Off.

HiT entertainment

A catalogue record for this book is available
from the British Library

ISBN 978 0 85733 851 8

Library of Congress catalog card no. 2015935805

Haynes North America Inc., 861 Lawrence Drive,
Newbury Park, California 91320, USA.

Published by Haynes Publishing,
Sparkford, Yeovil, Somerset BA22 7JJ, UK
Tel: +44 (0)1963 442030
Website: www.haynes.co.uk

Design: Lee Parsons

Illustrations:
John Lawson – pages 8–25, 30–33
All illustrations © 2009 Gullane (Thomas) LLC.

Printed in the USA by Odcombe Press LP,
1299 Bridgestone Parkway, La Vergne, TN 37086

Haynes Publishing
www.haynes.co.uk

AUTHOR: CHRIS OXLADE

CONTENTS

6 **Welcome aboard**
Come and meet the characters
on the Island of Sodor

8 **Thomas**
A closer look at
Thomas the Tank Engine

10 **How a steam engine works**
See how an engine like
Thomas works

12 **Driving Thomas**
Learn how Thomas' Driver
makes him go

14 **Gordon**
A closer look at a
tender engine

16 **Looking after engines**
How the Engineers look after
the engines on Sodor

18 **An engine changes**
How Henry was repaired
and refitted

20 **Percy**
A closer look at a
saddle-tank engine

22 **Building an engine**
How a steam engine like
Thomas is built

24 **Mavis**
A closer look at a
diesel engine

26 Lots more engines
Meet some of the other engines found on Sodor

28 Carriages and other friends
Not all of Thomas' friends on the Sodor Railway are engines

30 Trevor & Harold
A closer look at a traction engine and a helicopter

32 The tracks of Sodor
Learn more about the different parts of a railway track

34 Old and new engines
A look at how engines have changed over the years

36 Thomas' railway facts
Things you didn't know about trains

38 Thomas' Really Useful Words
Some useful train words and what they mean

WELCOME ABOARD!

Welcome to the *Thomas the Tank Engine Manual*!

And hello from Thomas and his friends.

This book is all about Thomas and the other engines that work on the Island of Sodor.

REALLY USEFUL FACT

Look out for *Really Useful Fact* boxes filled with fantastic Thomas facts.

STATION

Thomas has water tanks on each side of his boiler. That's why he is called Thomas the Tank Engine!

Thomas pulls his carriages Annie and Clarabel and freight trucks.

Thomas has six wheels.

Funnel

Dome

Boiler

Coupling for pulling trucks and carriages

Buffers for pushing trucks and carriages

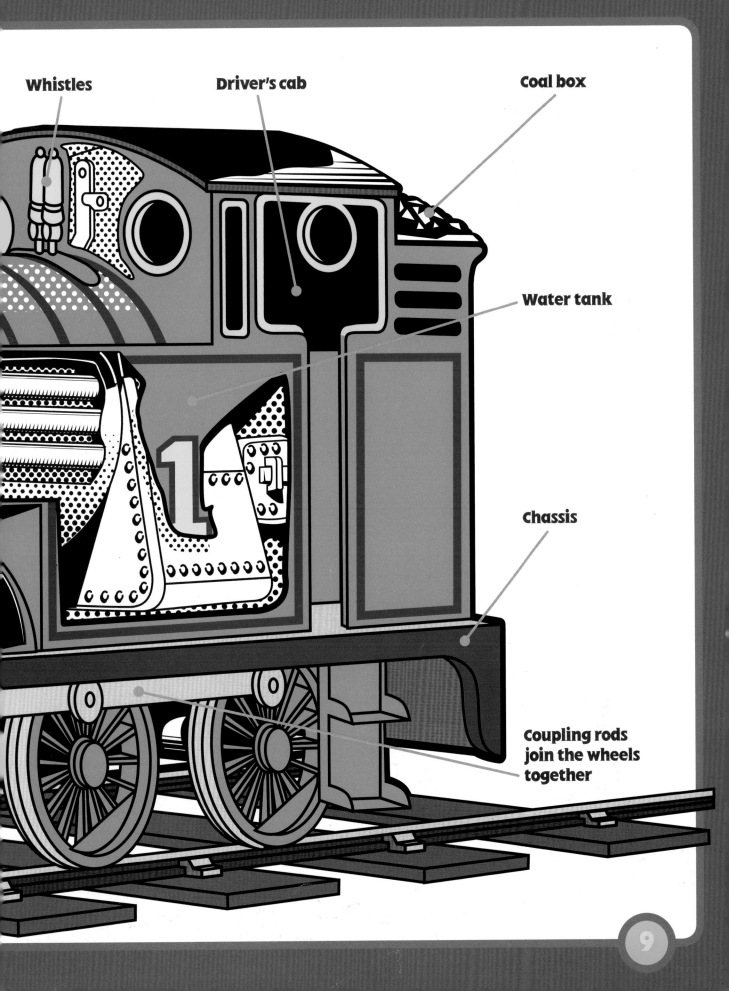

Whistles

Driver's cab

Coal box

Water tank

Chassis

Coupling rods join the wheels together

The Fireman starts a fire in Thomas' firebox. He shovels in coal to make the fire burn fiercely. The fire boils water in the boiler to make steam.

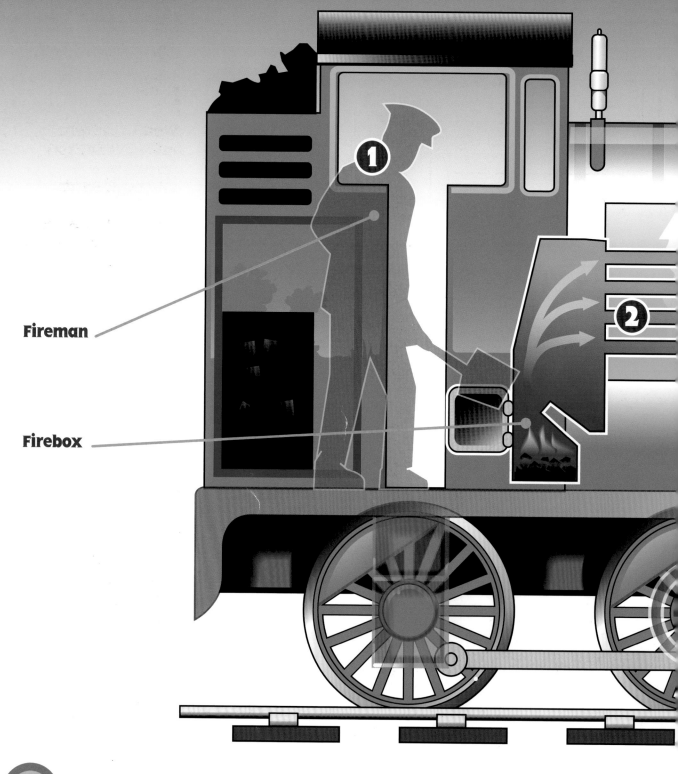

Fireman

Firebox

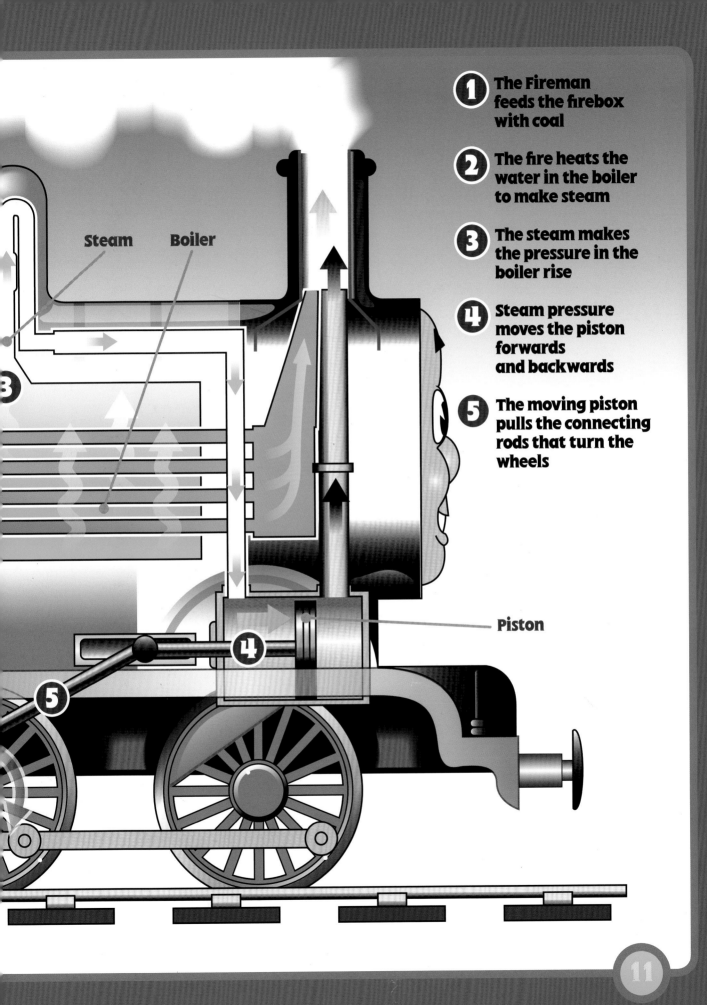

Steam **Boiler**

1 The Fireman feeds the firebox with coal

2 The fire heats the water in the boiler to make steam

3 The steam makes the pressure in the boiler rise

4 Steam pressure moves the piston forwards and backwards

5 The moving piston pulls the connecting rods that turn the wheels

Piston

Thomas the Tank Engine has two crew members.

His Driver makes him speed up and slow down, and go forwards and backwards.

His Fireman looks after his fire and boiler.

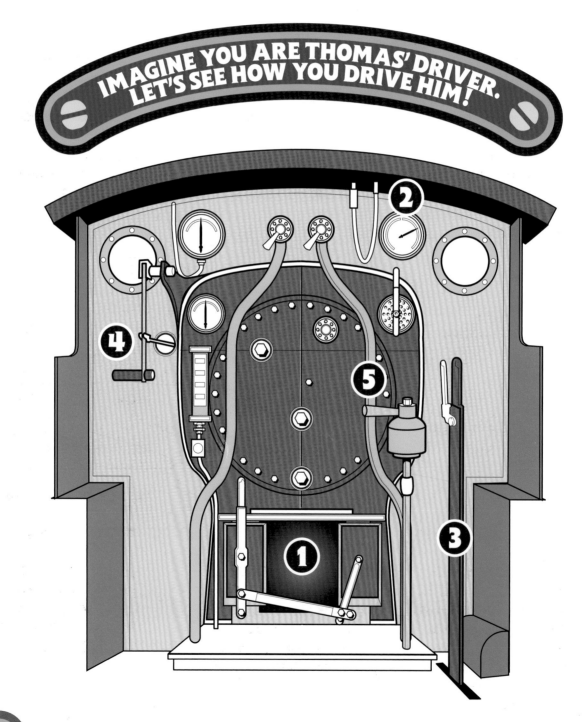

IMAGINE YOU ARE THOMAS' DRIVER. LET'S SEE HOW YOU DRIVE HIM!

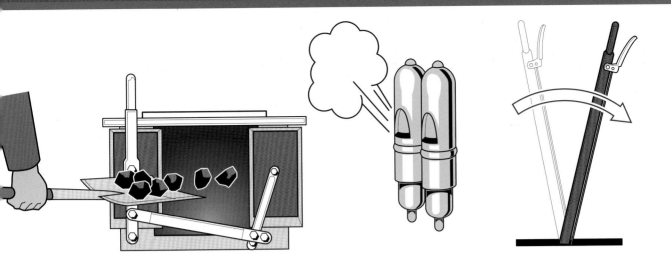

1 The Fireman starts a fire in Thomas' firebox. He shovels in coal to make the fire burn fiercely. The fire boils water in the boiler to make steam.

2 Pull on the handle to make Thomas' whistle peep. The whistle warns people that Thomas is about to move.

3 There is a long pole coming up from the floor. It is called the reverser handle. Push it forwards.

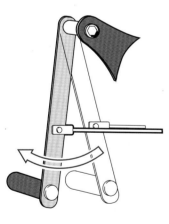

4 There is a long rod high up in front of you. This is the regulator. Pull it out to make steam rush into the cylinders. You can hear the chuff chuff of the steam in the funnel. We're off!

5 We're coming to a station. Time to stop! Push the regulator forwards. Now turn the brake levers to work the brakes and make Thomas slow down.

Thomas needs some more water. Stop at the water tower. The Fireman puts the hose into Thomas' water tanks.

Gordon is the fastest and most powerful engine on Sodor's railways. He pulls the passenger Express train.

Gordon is a tender engine. He pulls a tender with coal and water for his fire and boiler.

Gordon has twelve wheels. His tender has six wheels.

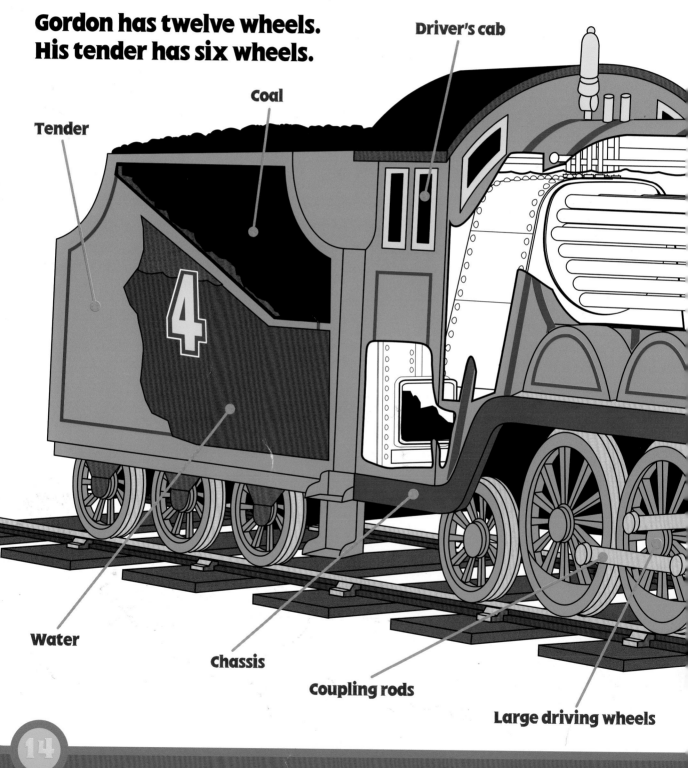

Driver's cab

Coal

Tender

Water

Chassis

Coupling rods

Large driving wheels

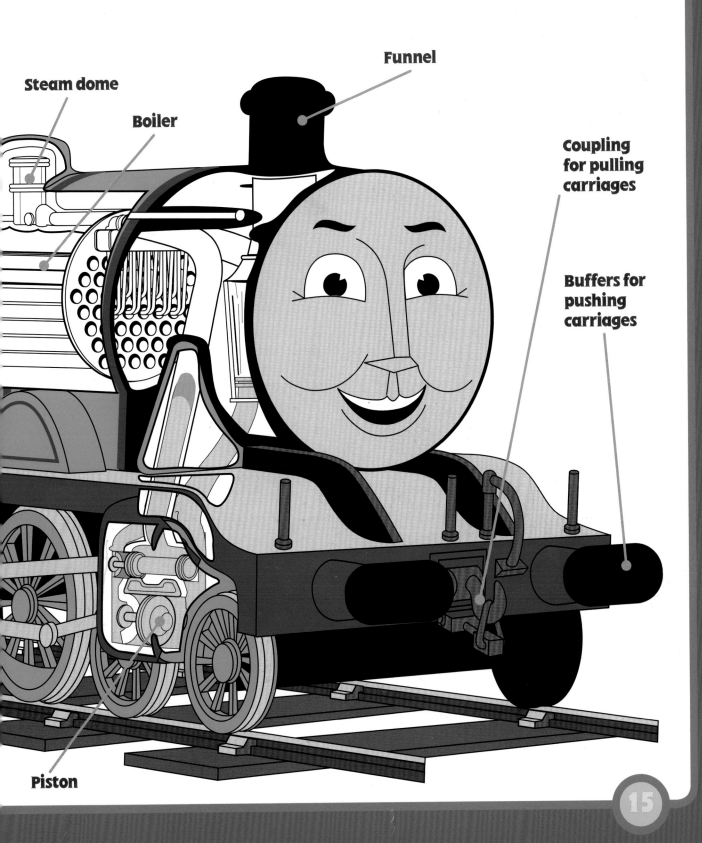

Steam dome

Boiler

Funnel

Coupling for pulling carriages

Buffers for pushing carriages

Piston

The engines of Sodor are looked after carefully to keep them working. They are cleaned every day, and if they go wrong, they visit the engine repair shed to be fixed.

The Drivers and Firemen polish and wipe pipes and paintwork to keep them gleaming.

Engineers check that all the parts are working properly. They tighten any loose nuts and bolts. They squirt on oil and grease to keep everything moving smoothly. Oil makes the wheels turn easily.

Thomas and the other engines work hard. Sometimes their parts wear out or break. Engineers take off the worn-out or broken parts and replace them with new ones.

Every few years the engines are overhauled. That means they get new parts and a fresh coat of paint to make them look smart.

The Engineers are
giving Thomas a
new set of wheels

Henry is a hard-working engine who pulls coaches and trucks. But he wasn't always so Useful. Here's the story of how Henry changed.

Henry was built as an experiment. His firebox wasn't big enough. So when he arrived on Sodor he could not make enough steam to go fast or pull heavy loads.

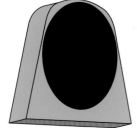

Henry's old firebox

One snowy night Henry was pulling The Flying Kipper. He went over some frozen points that sent him into a siding at high speed. He crashed into another train and was badly damaged.

Henry was sent to the Mainland to a big engine repair shed at Crewe. Henry was repaired, and The Fat Controller decided to give Henry a new, bigger firebox too.

Henry's new firebox

When Henry got home everybody was excited to see his new firebox. Now Henry has no problem making lots of steam.

Percy is a small engine who often works in the quarries and mines on the Island.

Percy is a saddle-tank engine. His water tank sits around his boiler, like the saddle on a horse.

He has four big wheels.

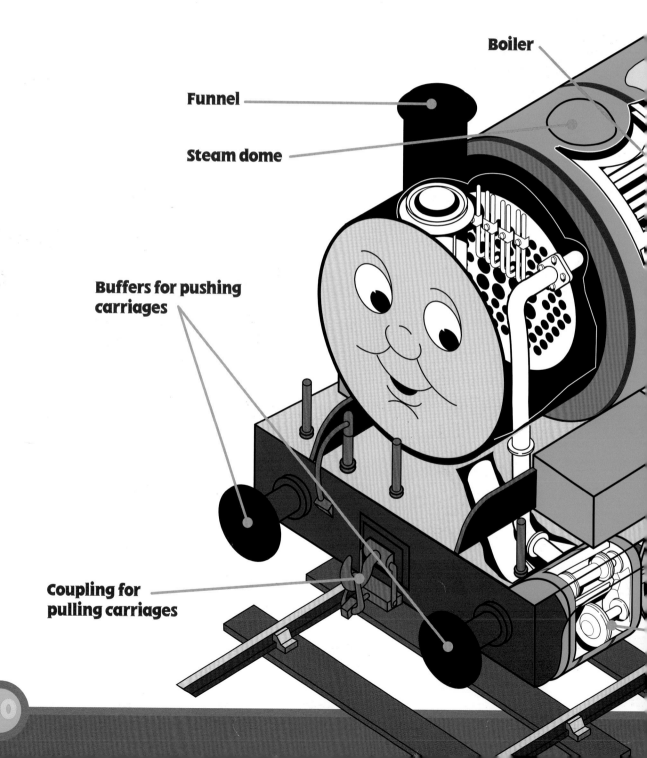

Boiler

Funnel

Steam dome

Buffers for pushing carriages

Coupling for pulling carriages

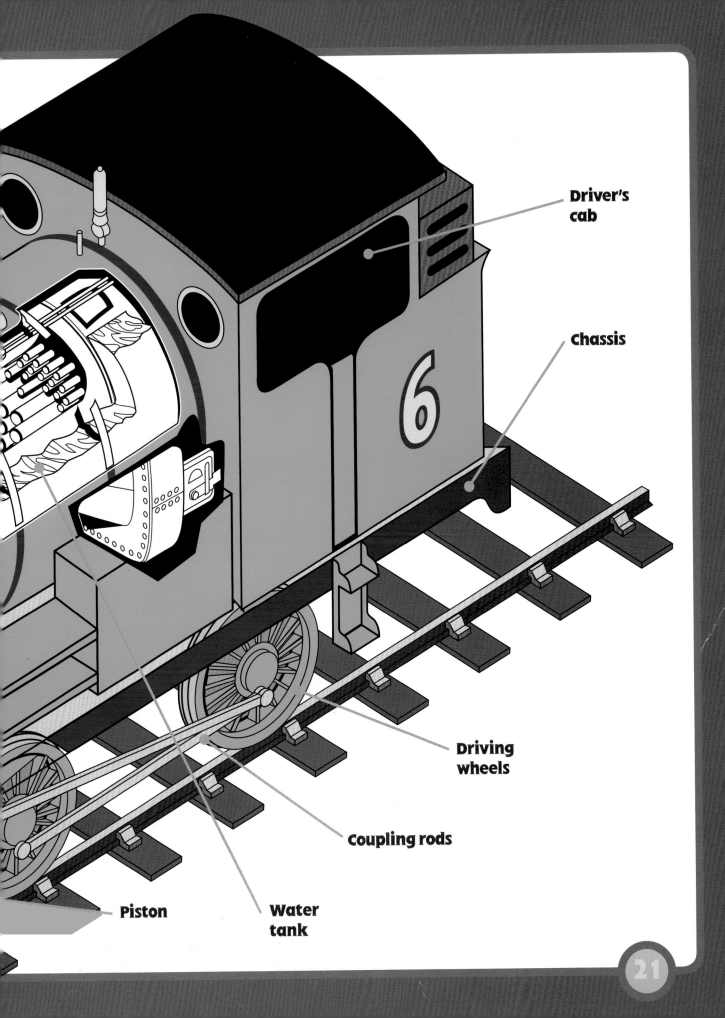

Driver's cab

Chassis

6

Driving wheels

Coupling rods

Piston

Water tank

Follow these steps to see how an engine is made. The metal pieces are made and joined together in a huge factory.

1 The chassis is the frame of the engine. All the other parts are attached to it.

2 The cylinders and smoke box are fitted into the chassis.

3 The firebox and the cab are put on the chassis.

4 The boiler is made next. It is a giant cylinder made from curved sheets of metal. The boiler is joined to the chassis.

5

Next the engine's wheels are made. The wheels are joined to axles.

6

The engine is lowered onto its wheels.

7

The tender is attached to the engine. Finally the engine is tested to make sure it works.

23

Mavis is not a steam engine. She has a powerful diesel engine inside that makes her move.

Mavis is a shunting engine. She works hard at the Quarry, where she pushes and pulls trucks and carriages.

Mavis has six wheels which are joined together to help her move heavy loads.

Mavis has a cow-catcher. She uses it to gently push cows off the track when they get in the way.

Buffers for shunting

Coupling

Cow-catcher

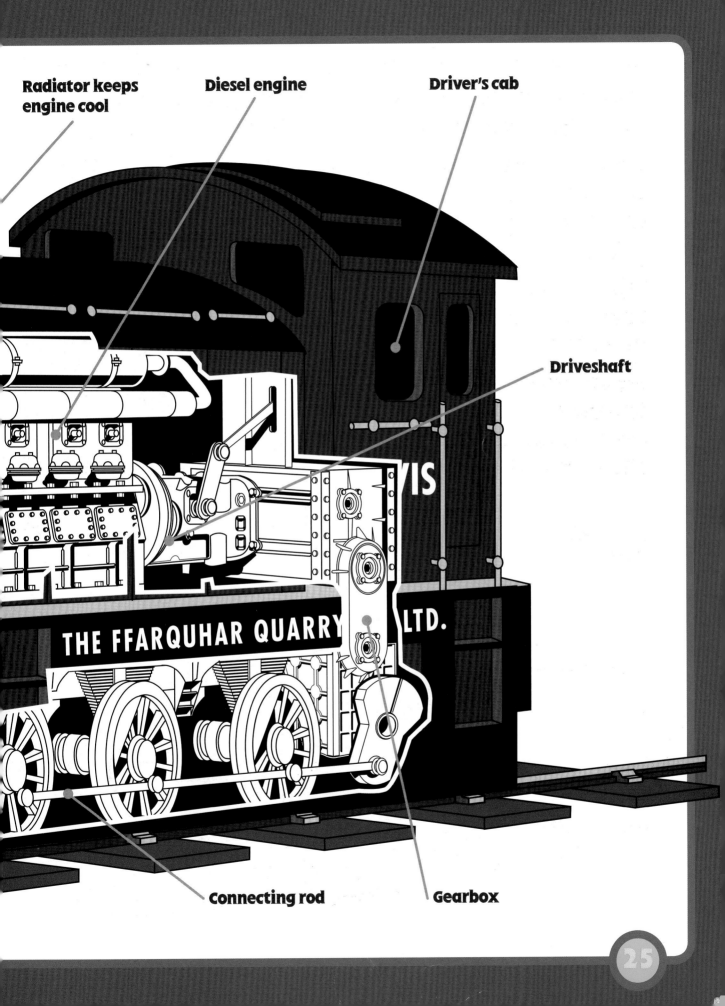

Radiator keeps engine cool

Diesel engine

Driver's cab

Driveshaft

THE FFARQUHAR QUARRY LTD.

Connecting rod

Gearbox

Let's find out about some of Thomas' friends on Sodor. They come in all shapes and sizes.

EDWARD
Engine number 2
Number of wheels 8

Edward is a tender engine. He pulls coaches and trucks.

> ⚙ **REALLY USEFUL FACT** ⚙
>
> **Edward and James are tender engines. Each one pulls a tender that is full of water for his boiler and coal for his fire.**

JAMES
Engine number 5
Number of wheels 8

James is a tender engine. He pulls coaches and trucks.

GORDON
Engine number 4 Number of wheels 12

Gordon is a big tender engine. He is the fastest engine on Sodor. He pulls the Express train.

> ⚙ **REALLY USEFUL FACT** ⚙
>
> **Percy is a saddle-tank engine. Saddle-tank engines have tanks for water over their boilers.**

PERCY
Engine number 6
Number of wheels 4

Percy is a saddle-tank engine. He pulls coaches and trucks.

HENRY
Engine number 3
Number of wheels 10

Henry is a tender engine. He pulls coaches and trucks.

MAVIS
Number of wheels 6

Mavis is a diesel engine. She works at the Ffarquhar Quarry, shunting trucks loaded with stone.

TOBY
Engine number 7
Number of wheels 6

Toby is a steam tram engine. He works on a quarry line and on Thomas' branch line.

Not all of Thomas' friends live on Sodor's railways.

ANNIE AND CLARABEL

Annie and Clarabel are passenger carriages that Thomas pulls.

CRANKY THE CRANE

Cranky works at the Docks, lifting cargo between ships and trains.

REALLY USEFUL FACT

Lots of Troublesome Trucks work at the Ffarquhar Quarry. They carry heavy loads of stone.

TROUBLESOME TRUCKS

The trucks carry all sorts of cargo on Sodor's railways. They work all over the Island. But they love to cause trouble!

ROCKY

Rocky is a special truck with a strong crane for lifting engines back onto the track.

ALFIE THE DIGGER

Alfie is a digger who loves working hard and getting mucky.

BERTIE THE BUS

Bertie is a single-decker bus. He carries passengers along the roads of Sodor.

Trevor is a traction engine. He's like a farm tractor, but he is also a steam engine like Thomas.

Trevor works in the Vicarage Orchard, where he pulls trailers of fruit and sometimes gives children rides.

Trevor has wide metal wheels that grip the ground and stop him sinking into the mud.

His steam engine turns a heavy flywheel that turns his wheels.

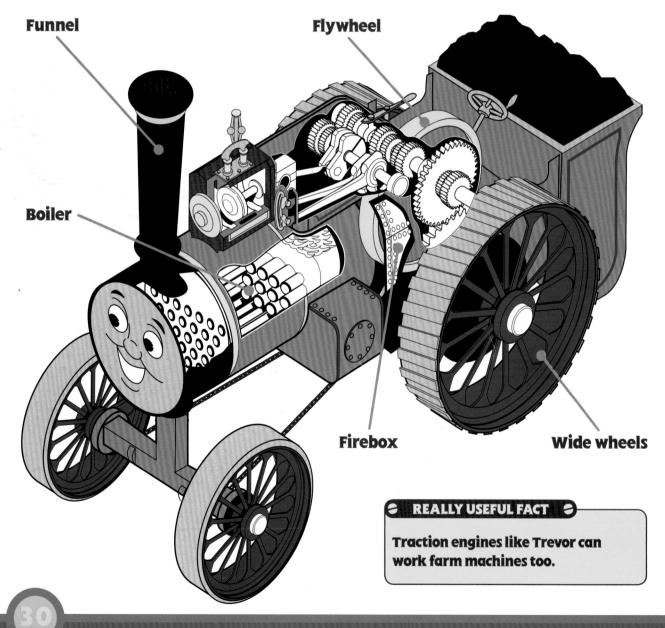

Funnel

Flywheel

Boiler

Firebox

Wide wheels

REALLY USEFUL FACT

Traction engines like Trevor can work farm machines too.

Harold is a helicopter, who is often seen flying over Sodor.

Harold's rotor spins round very fast. When it's spinning it lifts Harold into the air.

Harold has floats for landing on water and wheels for landing on the ground.

Pilot's cockpit

Main rotor

Tail rotor

Engine

HAROLD

Floats

REALLY USEFUL FACT

Thomas and the other engines call Harold "Whirlybird" because his rotor whirls round.

Sodor has lots of railway lines. The Main Line goes from one side of the Island to the other. Branch Lines lead from the Main Line into the countryside and to the coast.

TRACKS

Railway tracks have two strong metal rails. The rails rest on thick planks of wood called sleepers. Under the sleepers are stones called ballast.

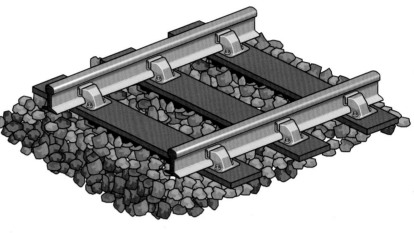

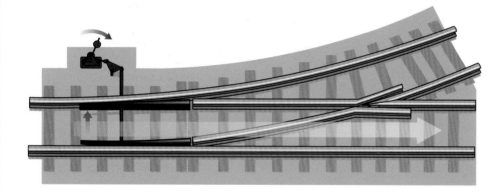

POINTS

Points let trains turn off one track onto another. You see lots of points at stations, where branch lines leave the main line, and in sidings.

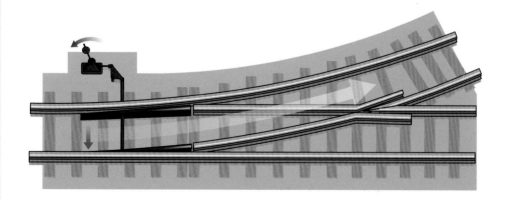

TURNTABLES

A turntable lets engines turn round and get from one track to another. The turntable at Tidmouth lets the engines get from their sheds onto the Main Line.

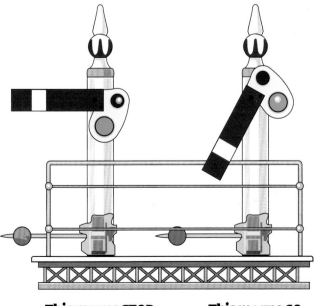

SIGNALS

Signals tell the engine drivers when to stop and when to go. They're just like traffic signals on the road. Trains often have to stop if there is another train ahead, or to wait for points to be changed.

This means STOP   **This means GO**

There are lots of different engines on Sodor's railways. Some are old and some are new. Here you can see what trains from the past and modern trains look like.

THE FIRST STEAM ENGINES

The first railway engines were made about 200 years ago. They are very old and don't work anymore.

FREDDIE ⑦

NARROW-GAUGE ENGINES

Narrow-gauge engines like Freddie were built about 150 years ago. They were very slow.

REALLY USEFUL FACT

Today the fastest trains are electric trains. They have big electric motors that turn their wheels. There are no electric trains on Sodor.

THE FIRST EXPRESS TRAINS

Engines like Emily were made about 100 years ago. Emily was built to pull express trains. She has two large driving wheels.

NEWER STEAM ENGINES

Later steam engines were big, fast and powerful, like Spencer. He has a smooth body to help him whizz along the tracks.

SPENCER

DIESEL ENGINES

Diesel engines are modern engines. They have a diesel engine, like the engine in a large car or truck, but much bigger and more powerful.

Chuff chuff! The noise of steam engines is made by steam coming out of their funnels.

Thomas works on his own branch line. It runs between Tidmouth and the town of Ffarquhar.

Shunting engines, such as Mavis and Bert, work in the sidings. They push, pull and sort wagons.

Thomas' whistle works by steam. When his Driver pulls a string, steam rushes through the whistle.

Sodor is an island. But the Main Line is connected to the Mainland. That's how Henry got to Crewe to be repaired.

Clackety clack, clackety clack! That's the noise of Thomas' wheels going over joints in the rails.

The Culdee Fell Railway is very steep. It has a special extra rail that the trains hold onto to stop them sliding down.

What are those black towers beside the track? They are water towers, holding big tanks of water for the engines.

The steam engines use up water in their boilers as they work. They often stop at water towers to refill their water tanks.

Harvey is a crane engine. If an engine comes off the rails, Harvey helps to lift it back on again.

ISLE OF MAN

Arlesdale Green

Ffarquhar Road

Arlesburgh West

Arlesdal

Hackenbeck

Haultraugh

Ffarquhar

Elsbridge

Tidmouth

Toryreck

Knapford

Dryaw

Crosby

Wellsworth

10 MILES

SODOR

ENGLAND

Culdee Fell Summit

Skarloey Road

Shilah

Kirk Machan

Rheneas

Skarloey

Barrow

Vicarstown

Glennock

Norramby

Abbey

Cronk

Kildane

Cros-ny-Cuirn

Maron

Crovan's Gate

Suddery

Kellsthorpe Road

Rolf's Castle

Brendam

Kirk Ronan

BOILER
Part of a steam engine. This is where water is heated to make the steam that moves the engine's wheels.

CHASSIS
Part of a steam engine. It is a strong frame that all the engine's other parts are fixed to.

COUPLING
A hook and chain used to join engines, carriages and trucks to each other.

DIESEL ENGINE
A railway engine with a big diesel engine that moves it along.

BRANCH LINE
A railway line that connects stations on the main line to other stations.

FREIGHT
Anything carried by railway trucks, such as parcels, wood, coal or ballast.

BUFFERS
Every railway engine, carriage and truck has buffers at each end. They stop the engines, carriages and trucks from bumping into each other.

CYLINDER
Part of a steam engine. Steam goes into the cylinder and pushes a piston backwards and forwards.

PISTON
Part of a steam engine that makes the wheels turn. Steam pushes it backwards and forwards inside the engine's cylinders.

WATER TANK
A container on a steam engine that stores water for the boiler.

QUARRY
A place where rocks are dug out of the ground.

SIDINGS
Railway tracks where carriages and trucks are stored when they are not being used.

TENDER ENGINE
A steam engine that pulls a tender behind it. The tender is full of coal and water.

FIREBOX
Part of a steam engine. This is where the fire burns to heat the water in the boiler.

SADDLE TANK
A water tank that sits over the top of a steam engine's boiler. An engine with a saddle tank is called a saddle-tank engine.

FUNNEL
A chimney on top of a steam engine where smoke and steam come out.

NARROW GAUGE
A railway with rails that are close to each other. On Sodor, the Skarloey Railway is a narrow-gauge railway.

1